A Fragile Gift of Love

A Fragile Gift of Love

Reba Boackle David

ISBN: Softcover   978-1-4797-6179-1
               Ebook   978-1-4797-6180-7

This book was printed in the United States of America.

To order additional copies of this book, contact:
Xlibris Corporation
1-888-795-4274
www.Xlibris.com
Orders@Xlibris.com
126190

Contents

With sincere appreciation to all who have shared their
Pain, Joy and Love with me.

He who has not looked on sorrow will never see joy.
Kahlil Gibran

Dedicated To My Father
Abraham Milton Boackle
August 15, 1905—November 19, 1987

Forward

As a parish priest for almost forty years and as a pastor for 30 years I have had to deal with the sadness of human life in various ways. In the face of grief, words fail and trite platitudes sometimes evoke anger in one whom we are trying to console. I have often felt helpless in the face of human loss and wanted to do more than extend the care and concern of a priest for a suffering member of his flock. Death, divorce, the loss of a pet can be especially difficult for children. The inability of children to properly express grief in the face of loss often leads to misbehavior and emotional issues.

Adults sometimes need help in overcoming loss and moving on with their lives. For many people the grief experience is an emotional trauma that needs attention in the same way that physical illness must be treated. Yes, some need professional help to get past their difficulties, but my experience is that support groups and the counseling by an individual who truly understands the grief process is most beneficial.

It was in the face of these realities that Reba David came into my life. She was not a professional counselor at the time. Her background was teaching and administration. It was her desire to help develop programs for a parish and parish school that would help minister to the special needs of loss and grief We no longer had to just say" I'm sorry for your loss" but now we could provide a way for both adults and children to deal with their grief. Reba went to became certified as a grief counselor. We would now program as a ministry of the parish, support groups for people dealing with grief and loss. I was later transferred and Reba would move on to another parish where she would continue and expand her ministry. Over the years, so many individuals have told me how much Reba helped them through the darkness of grief. The smiles on their faces revealed the success of what she had accomplished.

Reba David has spent over 20 years in grief ministry. Her experience with children and families in education led her to believe that more was necessary for students and adults to deal with the effects of grief and loss in families. Most of us are emotionally equipped with proper help to heal from grief. Individuals need to be led through the phases of grief to move toward healing. We should be able to recognize and help these individuals with whom we are in contact. How many are needlessly hurting because there is no one who understands their pain?

The wisdom gathered over her many years of working with people are expressed so well in the pages of this book. Reba as a woman of faith is able to express the hope we should have as Christians in the face of loss, as well as the practical aspects of dealing with our human loss.

These are the reflections of an intensely caring woman who has touched so many lives and brought people from the darkness of despair to the light of hope.

Compassion is a Christian virtue which unfortunately can become misguided because the person offering compassion is more concerned about feeling good about what they are doing. True selfless compassion is expressed in these pages.

I would hope that those reading this book will comprehend its meaning in light of a woman who desires more than anything else, to offer hope to suffering people.

Monsignor Victor P. Ciaramitaro

Monsignor Ciaramitaro is presently Pastor of St. Michael Catholic Church in Memphis, Tennessee.

A Fragile Gift of Love

It was a normal October night in a small Mississippi town. A town where everyone took care of each other, where ones problems were helped by those able to render a helping hand. Here a good deed was not forgotten. There were shirt factories, pea picking Saturdays, a small movie theater, a volunteer fire department, a consolidated school—where one entered the first grade and finished the twelfth grade—a large three story building.

My parents opened a small retail clothing store there some fifty years earlier. The night of October 25th, 1984, my father fell while helping my Mother, who had been on a walker for a number of years. This fall left him with a cracked spine—one that would keep him bed-ridden for the rest of his life. Never would the life of any member of our family be the same. Never would the small store be opened again.

As you may know in a small town many people would charge what they needed and my parents were always willing to help anyone in need. There was also a large lay-a-way in the store. Closing the store without prior notice left many customers with outstanding balances on their accounts, as well as items in the lay-a-way.

The credit card boxes, two very large long ones and all the lay away items were brought to our home. My parents said, "The customers know where we live and they will pay and they will come for what they have in lay away." Some three years later when my Dad died there were no charges left in the two boxes and all the lay aways had been paid out and picked up.

My parents had great faith in God and in their customers. Over the years they helped many people and felt like these same people would not forget them. The funeral homes in town would call my parents when they needed clothes in which to bury people. My parents never refused. They were always told to come and get whatever they needed.

It was my parents' philosophy that you always have enough to share with anyone who is in need.

Even though I lived two hundred and fifty miles from home, I would cook extra during the week, freezing enough to take home and on Friday after work I would go home to help over the weekend.

Several years prior to closing the store, a young butcher in town lost his home and all its contents in a fire in the middle of the night. In a small town news spreads quickly. My Dad had my Mom go to the grocery store to ask the butcher to come to the store when he got off work.

Robert came in and my Dad told him he had heard that he had a fire and lost everything during the night. He told my Dad he had, but he saved his family. My Dad than said "Robert, take whatever you need." He looked at my Dad, and said, "I didn't have any insurance". Dad replied, "I didn't ask you or expect you to pay for anything. Just put what you need on the counter and I'll help you load it in your truck."

Even though this happened many years before my Dad had to close the store, Robert did not forget. As soon as he heard my Dad had to close the store and was going to be confined to bed he came to our home. He asked if he could come on his lunch hour and shave, bathe and help take care of my father's needs. Robert did this for three years, never missing a day.

Each time I visited my parents I could see my Dad decline. His pain increased, his appetite was not good. All my life I had been very close to my Dad and to see him failing in health really hurt me and I began to think, how was I going to handle his death. How was I going to cope?

Thus began my journey of joy, hope, and love. My life and my own family's life was changing. My search for help for me was in vain. There were no support groups in Memphis and I knew I was going to need help. Having been an educator for thirty three years, I felt like I could learn and help myself, not knowing at the time, I would help hundreds of people as well as train close to six hundred people to offer their support to those in need.

The summer of 1987 I went to Loyola in Chicago to see what I could learn, having read about a course being offered there. Little did I know at the time this would change my life forever.

The summer that I studied at Loyola was the last summer of my Dad's life. Prior to my going I talked about what I wanted to do. He thought that it was good and I should do it remembering whatever I started I had to finish. I told him I would not be able to come home for a few weeks. He felt like he and Mom would be fine. I left for Chicago, not realizing the work I was learning would change my life. A ministry which I would devote the next twenty three years of my life.

Two nights before I was to return home, I saw a notice on the bulletin board, after the night session, for me to call home. Scared, I called and Mom said, "If you want to see Dad alive, you must come now". How could I go home, nine o'clock at night, two more days to go, to be certified. I was angry, so angry; I ran for hours along Lake Michigan, crying, screaming at God, how He could do this. At last I went to my room, knelt at the foot of my bed exhausted. Praying, praying. I fell asleep. The sun shining through the window woke me the next morning. I ran downstairs, called Mom. She said, "it is a miracle, Dad is sitting at the kitchen table"! How could I have not trusted God?

How could I have doubted and not trusted God? My Dad lived five more months.

Grief changes ones life like nothing else. Once a loved one dies, a person is never the same. However, there is hope. God's love is a love that survives any loss. Love is stronger than death. Tears are the silent language of grief.

We are never ready for a loved one to die. We miss them the rest of our life—our memories together become so precious. Remember grieving is a beatitude "Blessed are they who mourn for they shall be comforted".

You can no longer be who you were before death entered your life. No one can teach us how to grieve because no two people grieve the same, not even over the same person. The relationship we had with the person before death is a great barometer of how we grieve that persons' death.

You will become more compassionate, more caring, more sensitive. You become a better person because death is a wonderful teacher and it leads us to become the person God intends us to be.

Like nothing else death changes a person. That is one reason our friends often change; they want us to be the way we were before death entered our life. I am sure you have often heard the saying; "until one walks in the shoes, one does not truly understand". They want to know when will we get better, when will we return to our old self. So our circle of friends changes.

However, there is no timetable for grief. Time by itself does not heal. It is what we do with the time. We must not allow ourselves to have pity parties for that is not what our love one would want for us. Your happiness is what your love one would want for you. Work with your grief and with an attitude of happiness.

Grief is an expression of love. Just because a person dies, it does not mean our love dies. Remember love is stronger than death. A part of who we are dies with that person and a part of who we become is part of the person who died.

When my Dad died I did not think I could live without him. Soon I came to realize so much of who he was lived in me. He and I shared our birthdays. I was born twelve minutes after his birthday. Our little joke was "I was a disappointment from the beginning".

We are no longer the person we were when our loved one died. Grief is very personal. Grief expresses the love we feel for the person who has died. Death is painful. We have a void in our heart. One must teach the mind and at the same time touch the heart in learning to process our grief.

We know that death is a mystery. It makes us face our own mortality. Yet, it teaches us so much. The death of a loved one is very painful. We have no choice when our love one dies. It is out of our control. We do have a choice in healing ourselves. It is the hardest work we will ever do. No one can do it for us. Even though grief is unique to each person it can be shared and a new and deeper understanding of life can emerge. I have found that death even has purpose. We must seek it. We must discover it, for it does come.

On November 19th, 1987 when that phone call came I knew. I was never going to see my Dad alive again. Dad prepared me the week before when I was leaving. He called me into his room three times before I left. He had never done that before. This was unusual for him to do. It was a Sunday afternoon and I was preparing to return home to Memphis. He thanked me for coming telling me he knew how hard it had been for me over the past three years. He wanted me to know he appreciated the love and support I had shown him and Mom. During the second time Dad reminded me to be careful and to call when I arrived home. It had begun to rain. The last time he called me into his room he kissed me one more time and he said, "remember how much I love you". He knew and I began to realize he was telling me goodbye for the last time.

It took me longer to get home than usual. I found comfort in the rain, for I felt God was crying with me. He understood my tears. That was the last time I saw my Dad. He died the next Thursday, four days before my middle son's birthday and one week before Thanksgiving. He knew this would be the last time we would see each other.

Many times the person knows they are dying and will let those they love say their goodbyes. I cried and it sprinkled rain the entire four hour drive home.

Nothing can take away the pain of losing someone you love. You cannot bring them back. You must acknowledge the pain, lean into it. Grieving makes one a stronger and richer person. You have suffered a crushing loss, you hurt. Often you feel you are going crazy. You are unsure of what is happening to you. You miss the one you love. You are lonely. All love leads to suffering.

Grief is good when it puts people in touch with God's goodness. "The Lord is close to the broken hearted: and those who are crushed in spirit He saves" (Psalm 34:19).

While the experience of grief work is difficult, slow and wearing, it is also enriching and fulfilling. Some of the most beautiful people I have known are those who have known suffering and loss and have found their way out of the depths. These people have an appreciation, a sensitivity, an understanding of life that fills them with compassion, gentleness and a deep loving concern for others.

You are not alone. God has promised "I will never forget you I have carved you in the palm of my hands" (Isaiah 49:15-16) The pain will go away, but will return again and go away for a longer period of time Your life will shape itself around those comings and goings. The loss will always be there and in the process of grief you learn to accept that loss. Endings will bring new beginnings. You have endured a crushing blow, a great emotional stress. God will give you all the strength you need. Listen to him in the silence of your heart. He is speaking.

The word goodbye—originally "God be with ye" or "Go with God" is a significant part of the going. Goodbyes are a blessing of love, for with God our love one is never alone. To say goodbye helps you to experience the depth of your human condition.

It enables you to have a better understanding of life, a greater compassion and wisdom, with a deeper courage to continue the journey which will eventually take us all to our eternal home.

Once we learn to say goodbye in death we truly learn to say "go and be with God". The God who promises to wipe away our tears, to hold us close and fill our emptiness. Every goodbye has some suffering. The greater the parting the deeper the pain. The greater the loss, the more severe the emptiness that accompanies it. View your suffering from the perspective of resurrection, believe there is something beyond death. There is hope, strength and power in resurrection at work in each of us.

God understood my sorrow, He wept with me, He assured me joy would return. Trust Him. God gives you the wisdom and the courage to do what you must. Cry, for tears are the holy water God gives you to help you grow through your grief. Water brings life to everything and everyone. Let your tears bring an honest prayer to the heart and to the ears of God. You are not lacking faith when you feel sorrow. There is no end to God's power in helping you heal. Remember God's love is unconditional.

Having been given a strong faith through my parents as I was growing up has helped me in every walk of my life. As a child there was no Catholic Church in our little town. We had no family car until I was twelve years old. Never the less every Sunday morning our family walked five miles to the Greyhound bus station, rode the bus twenty five miles, then walked to a near by Catholic Church, attended Mass and then reversed our journey back home. This was every Sunday morning, rain or shine. The faith that was taught us by word and example has carried me through life.

At the age of twelve a missionary priest stopped by our house to inquire about having Mass in our home for the Catholics in town. Of course, my parents were thrilled. For the next eighteen months Mass was held in our home. Each week more people came and soon we were looking for a larger place for Mass. We found a room over the drug store and it wasn't long before a church was built. Than came the rectory and lastly a parish hall.

With the death of my Dad I found the need to help others understand and work through the process of grieving. I have found that grief work is the hardest work one must do in life. When someone we love dies life changes forever. Grief like nothing else changes the way one looks at life. The journey through grief takes one through many different phases. One needs to realize these phases are normal as well as necessary.

You will be on this journey working your way through the process for a number of years. We come to love over many years and our grief which expresses that love will last for many years. It is normal and human for our emotions are the essence in the healing process.

When recovering from grief the hardest step of all is facing the reality of death. There is no way to make this easy. Grieving is natures' way of healing a broken heart. There is a void in your life, a hole in your heart.

You now have a choice. You must grieve. You deal with your inner feelings. You express and resolve them. In order to do this you begin to understand the phases through which you come through many times to arrive at your new life. It is important to remember, you will pass through these phases many times and in no special order. Choose not to bury your feelings for they will come back. Grieving phases are necessary for your healing. Going THROUGH the phases of grief is essential. In time, the discovery of "rebirth" justifies the pain.

Nothing could have prepared me for that phone call on that cold November morning—eleven minutes to eleven. Dad is in the hospital. I was working in a church office. I went to church. I prayed. I knew that God knew what my Dad had been through the last three years. I know that God is merciful and in the silence of my heart, knowing and trusting Him to do what was best for my Dad. When I returned to the office, the call came Dad had died.

Everyone expresses their emotions to life's greatest hurt in different ways. One may cry or become very quiet. One may not cry at all. Whatever one feels is all right. Feelings are not right or wrong, good or bad. They are just feelings. We must not place band-aids on our wounds trying to be strong. God gives us strong shoulders on which to carry our crosses. He gives us the shoulders of others on which to cry. You do not have to be strong all the time. Death forces us to unwrap love, find pain, face anger and loneliness. Do not be afraid to mourn. With God you will grow strong in broken places.

Once one has begun to cope with life's changes, one is able to move forward with hope into the future God gives you. We rejoice in our suffering, because we know that suffering produces perseverance. Perseverance, character and character, hope. (Romans 5:3-4)

The Phases of Grief

The first emotional response to the death of a love one is shock. When in shock pain is numbed. It is as if God has provided an anesthetic. You become numb all over. Emotions may be out of control. Shock is a gift from God which may last a couple of days, weeks or even longer. Shock protects you from the full impact of the loss. Death is almost always a shock. Even though I knew my Dad was going to die the last time I saw him I did not want to believe it happened.

Denial is the first phase of the grief process. It is the most common emotion present at the time of death. One refuses to believe that it has happened. One believes that if I do not accept the fact it will not be true. We tend to deny anything too painful or upsetting in life, and death is at the top of the list.

Denial is natural for one bereaved. One stays in this phase for a time. We must have time to assimilate bad news. It is possible to stay in the phase too long. Grief is a unique process. Grief has no time table. So much depends on what we do with the time and how we process our grief.

One may put on a mask and say "I'm fine", you want everyone to think you are alright. You know inside you are hurting. It is difficult to talk about death. Much of the denial comes in not wanting to let go of the one you love.

Denial is normal, and one needs to pass through denial on the journey. Feelings that are buried too deep within come back years later. One must not bury feeling because it leads to depression. It is easier to bury feelings than to acknowledge them. One must acknowledge and lean into feelings no matter how painful.

Another phase of the grief process is anger. Anger often has no boundaries and is expressed any time at anything or anyone. You may be angry at the person that died, at doctors and even with God. Anger makes us miserable when not acknowledged. How we use anger is what is important. When denied, anger leads to resentment and self destruction, emotional, physical and spiritual behavior.

Understanding anger allows one the expression of fear. We express anger when we are hurt. We express anger when we are afraid of being hurt. We express anger when we feel we are in danger of being hurt. Often anger brings feelings of guilt and shame. To the contrary anger when used constructively is a healthy reaction. Feelings are not right or wrong, good or bad, they are just how one feels. It is important what one does with their feelings. The choice is yours. God gives man free will. You can turn to Him and use this occasion to grow in His love.

Bargaining, one's attempt to exchange something we are willing to give up, for that which we want to keep, is another phase in the grief process. We are attempting to postpone the inevitable. "What if" and "if only" go hand in hand with bargaining. It is a response to how things might have been or how we might have reacted. The truth is one must come to terms with that which one has no control. Yet we pray for miracles and bargain with God. Bargaining preys only on our fears and vulnerabilities. God understands and loves us unconditionally.

When one can't cope, life often spins out of control and one is overwhelmed. Depression comes when the reality of the death weighs heavy on our hearts. Changes in mood, attitudes and temperament occur during this difficult time. Life becomes a tug of war with emotional ups and downs. We become reactive rather than responsive to everyday pressures.

You are weathering a terrible storm. You feel alone. You feel no one understands. You need to take this burden outside yourself, express your feelings to someone you trust. It is normal to experience depression after the death of someone significant in your life. Feelings of despair need not become a defeating way of life. When you begin to realize that you are not alone, you will gain a new awareness of the presence of

God. God knows the emotions that are churning inside of you. God suffers with you. This may be the first time in your life that you create a personal relationship with God from which you can draw strength and comfort. Feelings of hopelessness are often experienced with a sense of life beyond our control. It is your choice and you must move yourself from hopelessness to hope.

Hope returns when you start to reach for it. One begins to accept the reality through reaching out, getting support and working through depression. We begin to say to ourselves "tomorrow is going to be better, and I will work to make it better."

When you have learned to live with the changes in your life you come to accept the reality of life. It is important to go through all the phases many times in many ways.God gives you everything you need. He is always with you. You are never alone. You begin to remember your love one with all the love you shared in life.

Remember all the phases you go through in grief are important. You do not want to go around them or try to bottle them up. You may go in and out of them many times. The path may be jagged you may feel like a yo-yo. Everything you feel is a necessary part of the healing process. Allow yourself to feel each emotion. Express your feelings in ways that will not harm you or others.

Acceptance brings peace and a realization that God is always there to help you over the rough spots. God's love for you is a gift. All one must do is open your heart and let Him in. God speaks in the silence of your heart, are you listening?

Our Feelings

My life would never be the same. My Dad was such a large part of my life. Grief is an expression of love. I knew that my life was changed and I could never be who I was when he lived. Everyone at one time or another, in one way or another suffers when someone they love dies. Most of us will suffer more than once in our lifetime. We are never ready. Love is the beginning, for our real adventure begins when we love. Life ties one together, not death.

Nothing we have seen, done or learned in our life prepares us for the death of a love one. The pain will go away eventually. We must experience its coming and going. We will start to shape our life around this pain, beginnings and endings, hellos and goodbyes. The hurt grows dimmer and less intent with time. Grief is a sign of strength not of weakness. Grief work is the hardest work one will do in their life.

Allow yourself to feel all the emotions. You are beginning your journey of joy, hope and love. All you are feeling is normal and healthy. Don't be brave and ignore these feelings. GRIEVE. You can't make feelings go away by not acknowledging them. They hang around and linger longer when the grief is denied.

Death is the final cycle of life. Grief wears many faces. It is both laughter and sadness, anger and relief. Grief has no schedule. No two people grieve the same. Time does not heal. It is what we do with time that brings healing. You have to participate in the healing. Once one opens up to the grieving process the grief will begin to diminish. Will you forget your love one? No! You continue to remember with LOVE! Love is stronger than death.

Anger, guilt, sadness and relief, four traits that should be emphasized. If these feelings are not recognized it will delay ones response to the reality and the healing process. These reactions are normal on the grief journey. Many prefer not to talk or acknowledge these reactions to death. They feel it is wrong to be angry. They may feel relief at the death of their love one. If their love one suffered, relief is often felt for they suffer no more. Illness required much time and attention from the family. Death like nothing else changes us. We no longer are who we were before death entered our life.

Never be ashamed of crying. A tear is said to be the dew of compassion. Tears are a gift from God to express sadness when felt at the time of the death. Embarrassment and apology sometimes accompany this display of grief. People often say they are sorry when they cry. How can we help but cry when someone we love and miss are no longer with us?

Express all of your feelings. They are not right or wrong, good or bad, they are just feelings. Be patient with yourself and others. Learn to live again with all of your feelings. Thank God that you have love. God does not take love away from us. Love grows in yet another form. As Mother Teresa said, "Never let anything so fill you with sorrow that you forget the joy of Christ Risen".

Facing the death of someone we love is devastating. One is forced to adjust to changes never before experienced. We can never be the person we were before their death. Changes no matter how painful can always lead to personal growth. In the first few months after my Dad's death it was impossible to really focus on what I had to do. I knew that the holidays were coming and holidays were always important in our family.

Dad would always make such a big thing out of finding the right Christmas tree. Mom would play the piano and we would decorate the tree, singing carols, drinking hot cocoa.

Christmas was a busy time in the store. My Dad could wrap the most beautiful packages. People would come in and even ask if he could wrap gifts for them. It was a great time in our family. Many happy memories were made during the holidays. It was hard work in the store and everyone was tired but it was a good tired.

When Dad died I had already purchased his Christmas gifts. They were wrapped and were on the bed in the spare bedroom. I could not take them back to the store and say "my Dad died and I can not use these". What was I going to do? I came up with the idea that there were places where old people lived and they might not have anyone bring them a gift. So I decided to take them to St. Peter Nursing Home. Writing what they were on the outside and the sizes, I took them and asked that they be given to anyone who otherwise might not have anyone bring them a gift. This is a tradition I have carried on since the death of my Dad. When my Mom died three years later, I thought I would just add gifts for a lady. This way I still have the joy of purchasing something for them each year. I find so much joy in continuing this and it helps to keep their memory alive.

Friends may not know how to relate to you unless they too have experienced a close and personal death. They feel uncomfortable. They don't know what to say or do. The tension may cause them to avoid you. During grief we cry, we need to do a lot of talking with a lot of people to make all the necessary transitions. You miss the comfortable routine that once you shared with your love one. Your basic values do not change. Interest in certain things may never be the same. New doors open to things that you never thought of doing before. Life has new meaning for you. Your life is different. You have learned to face your loss and to believe in yourself again.

However, we must ask for help. Remember no man is an island. We need others to help us in our daily life. Support groups will help you over the rough spots. They teach you to cope with the various phases of grief on this long and painful journey.

Since I knew there were no support groups in Memphis, I choose to start them for I felt the need. Not only did I start a support group for the bereaved but I also began to train others to lead support groups. I started with one group and as a need would arise I would write additional ones. I have now written seven different ones for various needs. I have found purpose in the death of my Dad. I always would start by saying to God "here I am Lord, I come to do your will". He has always been there for me.

Emotions will start to circulate in your head. You wish there was a way to talk to your love one just for a minute. Of course, you can not do this, but you can write them a letter. When one is in grief, it is helpful to journal. Writing my Dad a letter was like talking to him. Keep a journal of your feelings, thoughts and your emotions in a notebook. It is very healing. The stress and the pain will move from your head and your heart to the blank sheet of paper. Just remember to use a pencil, ink smears and you will want to read what you are writing as you journey through grief. It is an interaction with others which allows one to give a little of our story away. Expressing our grief becomes easier with each entry.

One may be overwhelmed by circumstances over which one has no control. Live one day at a time to the best of your ability. "Lord, help me remember that nothing is going to happen to me today, that you and I together can not handle". You may even choose to write God a letter. He is always open to our prayers in any way.

In grief you will find emptiness, loneliness and tears. You become aware of the need for a closer relationship with God. Soon you come to know that God loves you. He is always there for you. Trust in God at all times.

One day you will look back and realize the death was a turning point in your life. The process of change is frightening. The most difficult human experience is letting go. Letting go does not mean forgetting your love one, burying memories or resigning yourself to the status quo. You face the past, move toward the future and remember with love. From birth to death, life is a process of letting go, a series of little "dyings", that take us to our own resurrection. In releasing things that prevent us from growing emotionally, spiritually and physically we are able to look ahead, to trust and to hope again. God will guide you in the right direction. You will rediscover the joy of life and growth again.

God works with you through sorrow to help you grow and mature as a human being. You learn from this experience of sorrow. God's promise is "your sorrow will be turned into joy".

This promise is given to us by Jesus. It has never failed for anyone who is willing to be blessed by the gift of joy.

Loneliness

The experience of loneliness is common to all who have experienced the death of someone we love. There is cruelty in death. It separates us from the touch and the voice of someone. We love them more, not less each day. It is not only the physical absence that makes us lonely but also the knowledge of permanence that makes our loneliness difficult to endure.

Death is a human experience which has no meaning of it own. Death takes all of its meaning from man. In death we find loneliness, painful and frightening. Loneliness can enhance dignity and maturity as well as beauty. Death opens new possibilities for love and tenderness.

In loneliness there is sensitivity, there is a deeper awareness of life. Loneliness is not something we choose for our self it is a given. Everyone at some time or another is lonely.

People complain of being lonely when someone special is no longer in their life. We live in loneliness when we fail to see the people who are already in our life. Our preconceived notions of how our friends should be closes the door to the presence of those who are in our lives. We need the presence of those who have walked a part of the journey with us. We need to leave the path open to realizing that every person we meet has something to add to our life. Not every person we meet will make the journey with us. Not every person will share with us to the same extent. All real living is a step that we make if our life is going to be enriched. We are called to see the people we meet with our hearts as well as our eyes. The need for human love which God has built into our being is strong. When we lose someone we love, no one can describe our sorrow.

Loneliness has a great purpose in our life. God did not plan loneliness for man. Man plotted it for himself through sin. The answer to loneliness is prayer. Union with God in prayer. Prayer is a constructive response to loneliness. Loneliness is an invitation to a deeper encounter with our self, God and others. One can not love another before he loves himself and God.

We are all made to the image and the likeness of God. We are human and we crave companionship. Everyone at some time or another is a little lonely. We need to be friendly and sincerely interested in other people. A pleasant word, a smile, a kind act the simple things that release us from our loneliness. Simple gestures of politeness and kindness lead to deep friendship and real love.

Loneliness can be a manageable companion by looking at your life through the eyes and experience of other people. Those who have been important to you and have made an everlasting mark on you as a person. There are many in your life when you take the time to look.

It is comforting to go through your love ones possessions, to touch, to hug and to even smell their clothes. Many people will make a memory box, or a memory drawer or perhaps a memory shelf. I have a beautiful memory shelf in our den that holds a picture of my parents, a pipe of my Dad's, Mom's thimble, their rosary beads. Place a candle you can light on special occasions. Count your blessings and remembering with love will help to fill your lonely spaces.

Your goal is to reach a point where you can be alone without being lonely. Enjoy your aloneness with peace and with tranquility. Your loneliness will soon come to find you new friends and new experiences. You will start to bloom and to grow. By being attentive to our life and developing a habit of noticing the meaning of life in others we will unfold new dreams and let go of broken dreams.

Eric Fromm claims that people trying to overcome loneliness have four tendencies. The first is to sink back into nature, to operate on instincts alone and abandon reason. To get lost in the crowd doing what everyone else is doing, without questioning motives so as not to stand out in the crowd, as yet another way. By throwing oneself into creative activity to produce something is the third tendency. In our deep fear of losing control and having to look at our loneliness, we fill up every hour of the day, so as we have no time to think about being lonely. Work on the job, at home, with volunteer organizations, stay so worn out that we have no time to grieve. We say "yes" to everyone who calls for help, not realizing that we need time for our self, time to grieve and feel the pain, no matter how much it hurts.

The only real solution to loneliness is active loving. He says this loving is three fold: loving our self, loving God, and loving others. Loving our self is the first step. If our self esteem is low, if we have no confidence in our abilities and gifts, then we can not love God or others.

The answer to loneliness is within, in your sense of self esteem and self. As you begin to know yourself, the next step is to take responsibility for what you find in yourself, take care of yourself, pick a goal and work to make it the center of your life.

When you become more comfortable with your identity, you will then reach out to others. You can learn from Thomas Merton who said, "The one who fears to be alone will never be anything but lonely, no matter how much he may surround himself with people".From emptiness, loneliness and tears you can come to an awareness of your need for a closer relationship with God. As you journey on the path of grief you will find many people who face experiences similar to yours that can help you. Always remember, no one need walk alone for the journey makes us one.

Coping With Loss

It takes a long time for our wound to heal. We have been robbed of someone very special in our life. As one goes through each phase you heal a step at a time. Just as broken bones become stronger where they break, you will become stronger as you heal. Before accepting your new life you must learn how to cope as you continue your grief journey. You are a witness to death. You must learn to do many new things on your journey. Some will be harder than others to accomplish. God will give you all you need for your journey. Family, friends and faith—the three f's. Without your faith, nothing else matters. God gives you all the graces you need in your life. He is involved in every heartbeat, call on Him. Listen to Him. Life is not a problem to be solved, but a mystery to be shared and to be lived. The spirit of God does not give us aspirins or tranquilizers but deep inner peace and serenity. This does not happen all at once, it takes time and patience. God always answers our prayers, maybe not the way we asked, but He sees our life here and in eternity. He always knows what is best for us. Give up and give into God's work in your life. Let go! Let God do His work.

Death is a time when you must give your all to God. You have given Him your dearest of persons-the ones you love so much. The void you feel, the pain can only be healed by the gentle touch of God.

Contact God through prayer. Let your prayers be ones of praise and thanksgiving. You can discover who you really are when you pray. God knows what is in your heart. Just be silent. Did you know if you take the letters in the word silent and rearrange them, you have the word listen? Many times we are so busy with the T.V., the cell phone, the radio, we have no time to listen. Prayer is listening and it takes time to find space and solitude in life. Learn to empty yourself so you can be open to God's word. You listen to other people, how often do you listen to God?

It takes courage and strength to face the enormity of our sorrow. We suffer. We hurt. Remember suffering does not last but having suffered last forever. Jesus said to St. Paul, "My grace is enough for you, my power is at its best in weakness". Suffering really is nothing but love. That is what we learn from the death of someone we love. We are in search of our self. We are grieving. We are also learning from our pain. How do you cope, how does anyone cope? There are many ways to learn to cope. You must find the ones that work for you and use them to help you through this time. Many people want you to smile all the time. Put on a mask and say you are fine. Doing this delays your healing. At times it seems easier to pretend all is well. Truth is our shadow. The more we try to deny that we are having a hard time, the harder it becomes and eventually will darken everything else. While you struggle to reassemble the pieces of your life, you need to understand what is taking place and learn to cope. Your life has become a puzzle and you must put the pieces back together again, one piece at a time. Verbalize your feelings so you can understand the emotions that are inside you. Many times you will need to ask for help because you are on task overload as well as emotional overload. It is possible to learn from your pain and grow from your experience of suffering.

The most important coping tool you have is your willingness to seek out those who are willing and caring, those who will listen and share with you themself. Life does not wait for grief, it goes on as you must do. You can not just grieve, you must grieve and grow. Personal relationships must move with you into a new understanding because you have changed. Your life has changed. You have the courage to grieve. Grieving people can find ways in their hearts to cope when they are given the chance to discover who they are becoming and if others are opening up their hearts to understand and to care. In your close interaction with others, you will always be seen as others think you are, seldom as you really are. You do the same. Hurt has a strange side effect. It can create closeness if you reach out to someone who cares, knows you and is willing to help you grow on your journey of grief.

The only way to handle grief so that it serves you instead of masters you is by looking it in the face with a willingness to go on with life. Life must be lived because it is worth living. When it has been shattered through death, it must somehow be rebuilt.

You know what it is to carry the person you love in your heart. Jesus speaks of the vine and the branches and of His abiding love. The abiding place is the heart, for there love is at rest and its place is secure.

Heaven for me would be to meet God in His heart at last, after a lifetime of meeting Him in mine and one day proud to hear Him say, "well done my good and faithful servant". You have used all the gifts I gave you.

In the early part of your journey in grief there are certain days which will bring more pain than others. These days hold special meaning to you as they remind you of an anniversary, a birthday or a special occasion. Remember I told you how Dad and I always shared our birthdays. He was born on August 15th and I was born on August 16th. He said "I was a disappointment from the beginning," because I was not born the day before. That was our little joke. You will feel alone. Special holidays that everyone observes, those that start months before the actual day. The first year these come up seem to be the hardest. Grief affects us all in different ways. It is going to be a time of pain and sorrow, of bittersweet memories.

There are two things that you need to remember at these special times in your life. First you will live in spite of the pain and the sorrow. The anticipation of these days is harder to endure than the actual day. Second, these days are coming so PLAN-PLAN-PLAN, what do you want to do on these days? Plan for yourself and with others who may be involved with you during this time. These plans do no have to be forever, they are not in cement and can be changed each year.

It is important on these days that you claim your pain, acknowledge it and lean into it. Cry, relive the illness, the death day, whatever else you must do to claim the pain. It is going to be there. Prepare yourself in what ever way you can.

On the death anniversary it was comforting for me to go over the visitors book, read over the cards and the notes I had received. Memories will come back to you that are so important. You will read things you missed at the time of the death. It is good to remember. It puts you in touch with who you are becoming on your journey. It will help you to let go of a certain period of your life and to start to look forward. There will be times when you are able to do this. Other times you feel you may need to take a few steps back. This is the roller coaster effect that you go through for years after the death of a love one. You may get stuck for a while no matter what you do. It is part of the process on your journey.

Life is changing and your needs now are different. Some days you may be able to accomplish a lot, other days you may find it hard just to get out of bed. You will find that if you can become involved and committed to doing things that will make a difference, even though it is hard, you will start the road to acceptance.

Remember tomorrow will never be the same as before the death of your love one. Take small steps before taking big ones. Take one day at a time. You will survive and it does become easier Try to live and to love each day, you have others in your life and you need to make every effort to enjoy and not hold back your love for them out of fear. You need to love, to care and to share your life to the best of your ability with others.

Memories

Memories are important to you and to others whose love is important to you. Memories touch and enrich our life and can help us and others we love to heal. Use pictures and videos to help you remember, look at gifts and mementos from your love one and recall the time you received these.

Some days will be more difficult than others, your birthday, your love ones birthday, family birthdays, holidays and family gatherings. Tears may swell and loneliness may come over you. Being aware that these days are coming and you have made plans that can really save you during these hard times. How do you want to spend the day, with whom do you want to be with, what things do you want to stay the same and what would you like to change? Go over all the things you feel with those you will be with on these days. Make them aware of your feelings and let them know that plans made for this year can be changed. Holidays are especially hard for me. Dad died one week before Thanksgiving, four days before my middle sons' birthday. My Mom died nine days before Christmas, three years later and four days after my oldest son's birthday. Remembering each of them in special ways has become a part of how I celebrate their life as well as the holidays.

Know that these special days will be filled with intense emotions. It helps to be with those who mean the most to you in your life today. Never pretend that you can handle it without planning. Take the time you need so that the day can bring joy as well as sorrow with ones you love and who love you. Tell your family how you feel, they may be shocked at first, but this shock can be good for them. It will help them to face the reality of the situation.

Can you learn to live with what you have instead of wishing for what was? You are not trying to eliminate the pain. You are learning to live with the pain. As you approach each special day do so with your head as well as with your heart. One grieves from the heart up, not the head down. Pray and ask God for strength during this difficult time. You will find not only strength but also courage.

Remember to be gentle with yourself during this time. Do not expect to do more than you know you will be able to do. Remember your love ones are hurting as well and they need tender loving care also.

Shopping is never easy for one in grief. Remember the way your love one liked to celebrate the day and try to do some of those things. Buy a gift for your absent love one and give it to someone who other wise would not receive a gift. It is in giving that we receive. Much joy will be spread by your sharing. You will be turning your sorrow into joy. When we share, love grows.

On special days light a candle in memory of your love one, their birthday, the anniversary of their death, holidays. Learn to celebrate the life they lived and the love they shared. Learn to look at joy and celebrate the things you had together.

When I was twelve years old, I made my Dad a promise. Each day I would look out of the window and say "this is the day the Lord has made, I will rejoice and be glad" (Psalm 118:22). No matter how shattered your life is there is still joy, hope and love. The morning after his death it was so hard to look out of that window, but I promised and I have not failed one morning.

The gifts of joy, hope and love are given to each of us by God. He is there for us in our sorrow, joy, fear, despair and peace. Try to be gentle with yourself. Remember your life has become different since the death of your love one. You will never be who you were before death entered your life. Their death will forever leave a void in your life. Some day you will look back and see their death as a turning point for you. Try to face the past releasing all negative feelings and allowing yourself to see the positive things in the present and in the future. Each life is a gift from God. Each of us have a purpose in life. Let your purpose be to live life to the fullest, thankful for the many blessings you have been given and ready to help others.

You are never alone in life. You have been given many friends, as well as other important people to help you with what ever obstacle comes your way. Some of these people will walk part of the way with you. You will walk part of the way with others. God will always be there to guide you. You will once again find joy, hope and love in your life. Use the grief that you experience as a stepping stone for new growth.

How long will you grieve? That is an individual matter. Living and expressing grief feelings is healthy and normal as well as necessary. When you come to acceptance it brings a peacefulness, a realization that God loves you so much and is always there for you. God's love for you is His gift to you. All you have to do is open your heart and let Him in. When you accept God's love, trust and faith, His guidance will become an important part of who you are becoming. It is always painful to say goodby to someone we love. There is no way to prepare you for what lies ahead on your journey. No one can lessen your hurt. You learn that you can live with the pain. You can learn to live with the memories. Remember with all of your love. Remember you will never be who you were before you started the grief journey. You will come to realize that there is much in your life that can be affirmed.

People who have known suffering and loss and have found their way out of the depths are the most beautiful people I have known. They are sensitive, understanding, gentle, compassionate and loving.

Let your journey of grief strengthen your faith and your love for others. Let your journey lead you to hold out your hand to another. There is risk in reaching out and opening our self to someone who is starting their journey of grief. Know God is working in and through you. As someone said in order to discover new horizons we must first loose sight of the shore. As you continue your journey, you will find and give joy, hope and love. May the Fragile GIFT of LOVE be what you remember most. May you find His Peace and His love always beside you.

When you are sorrowful look again in your heart and
you shall see that in truth you are weeping for that
which has been your delight.

Kahlil Gibran

www.ingramcontent.com/pod-product-compliance
Lightning Source LLC
Chambersburg PA
CBHW050342290526
45785CB00006B/2601